12 ways to make money online!!!

1. Affiliate marketing: This involves promoting other people's products and earning a commission for each sale made through your unique affiliate link.

2. Online surveys: Participating in online surveys can earn you money or rewards from companies seeking consumer opinions.

3. Freelance writing: Writing for blogs, websites, or online publications can earn you money based on the quality and quantity of your work.

4. Virtual tutoring: You can offer online tutoring services in various subjects and earn money through platforms such as TutorMe or Chegg.

5. Online selling: You can start your own online store on platforms like Etsy or eBay and sell handmade or vintage items.

6. Online course creation: Create an online course on a topic that you are knowledgeable about and earn money through platforms like Udemy or Skillshare.

7. Content creation: You can create content for social media platforms or blogs and earn money through ad revenue, sponsorships, or product placements.

8. Online consulting: If you have expertise in a specific field, you can offer online consulting services to clients through platforms like Clarity or JustAnswer.

9. Online bookkeeping: You can offer online bookkeeping and accounting services to small businesses and entrepreneurs.

10. Online programming: If you have programming skills, you can offer online programming services to clients through platforms like Upwork or Freelancer.

11. Online graphic design: If you have graphic design skills, you can offer online design services to clients through platforms like 99designs or DesignCrowd.

12. Online language tutoring: You can offer online language tutoring services to people learning a new language through platforms like Italki or Verbling.

Affiliate marketing: This involves promoting other people's products and earning a commission for each sale made through your unique affiliate link.

That's correct! Affiliate marketing is a performance-based marketing strategy where a business rewards affiliates for promoting their products or services and driving sales or leads. Affiliates promote the products by sharing unique affiliate links with their audience, which track any sales made through those links. The affiliate earns a commission for each sale made through their affiliate link. It's a popular way for bloggers, social media influencers, and website owners to earn passive income by promoting products or services that align with their audience's interests.

Online surveys: Participating in online surveys can earn you money or rewards from companies seeking consumer opinions.

Participating in online surveys can be an easy and accessible way to earn money or rewards by sharing your opinions and feedback with companies seeking consumer insights. Online surveys are conducted by businesses and research firms to gather information about consumer preferences, behaviors, and attitudes towards various products, services, or brands. The data collected from these surveys helps companies make informed decisions about their marketing strategies, product development, and customer service.

To participate in online surveys, you need to sign up for a survey panel or platform, such as Swagbucks, Survey Junkie, or Toluna. These platforms connect you with companies that are looking for feedback from consumers like you. Once you sign up, you will receive survey invitations via email or through the survey panel's website. The surveys typically take anywhere from 5 to 30 minutes to complete, depending on the length and complexity of the questions.

One of the benefits of participating in online surveys is the flexibility it offers. You can complete surveys from the comfort of your own home, on your own schedule. This makes it an ideal option for people looking to earn extra income without having to commit to a set schedule or location. Additionally, some survey panels offer different types of rewards for participating, such as cash, gift cards, or points that can be redeemed for prizes or discounts.

However, it's important to note that participating in online surveys is not a get-rich-quick scheme. The amount of money or rewards you can earn depends on the number of surveys you complete and the compensation offered by each survey panel. Some panels offer higher rewards for longer surveys, while others offer smaller rewards for shorter surveys. It's also important to be honest and thoughtful in your responses to the survey questions, as companies may disqualify you or stop sending you surveys if they detect inconsistent or low-quality answers.

Another potential downside of participating in online surveys is the risk of scams or fraudulent survey panels. It's important to research and read reviews of survey panels before signing up and providing personal information, such as your name, email, and address. Legitimate survey panels will never ask you for payment or sensitive information, such as your social security number or bank account details.

In summary, participating in online surveys can be a legitimate and easy way to earn money or rewards by sharing your opinions and feedback with companies. However, it's important to approach it as a supplemental income source and be cautious of potential scams or fraudulent survey panels. By finding reputable survey panels and being honest and thoughtful in your responses, you can earn extra income and contribute to the consumer insights that shape businesses' decisions.

Freelance writing: Writing for blogs, websites, or online publications can earn you money based on the quality and quantity of your work.

Freelance writing is a popular way to earn money online by writing content for blogs, websites, or online publications. Freelance writers can work with clients from all over the world and earn money based on the quality and quantity of their work. Freelance writing offers flexibility, as writers can work from anywhere with an internet connection, and often set their own hours.

To get started with freelance writing, you can create a portfolio of your writing samples and pitch your services to potential clients. There are various platforms available, such as Upwork, Fiverr, or Freelancer, where you can find clients looking for freelance writers. You can also reach out to individual blogs or websites that align with your writing niche and pitch them your ideas or services.

The key to success in freelance writing is to have strong writing skills and a niche or area of expertise that you can write about. Some popular niches include lifestyle, travel, personal finance, technology, and health. Freelance writers can also specialize in different types of writing, such as blog posts, articles, product descriptions, copywriting, or technical writing.

When working with clients, freelance writers typically negotiate their rates and terms of payment. Some clients pay per word, while others pay per project or per hour. It's important to establish clear expectations with clients regarding deadlines, revisions, and payment schedules to ensure a smooth working relationship.

One of the benefits of freelance writing is the potential to earn a consistent income. While rates vary depending on the writer's experience and the type of writing, freelance writers can earn anywhere from a few hundred to several thousand dollars per month. Additionally, as freelance writers build their portfolio and reputation, they can attract higher-paying clients and establish themselves as experts in their niche.

However, there are some challenges to freelance writing. One challenge is the competition from other freelance writers, as the field is highly saturated with writers from all over the world. It can also be difficult to find consistent work, as clients may have fluctuating needs and budgets. Freelance writers must also be disciplined and self-motivated, as they are responsible for managing their own time and meeting deadlines.

In conclusion, freelance writing can be a rewarding and flexible way to earn money online. By having strong writing skills and a niche area of expertise, freelance writers can attract clients and establish themselves as experts in their field. While there are challenges to freelance writing, with hard work and dedication, freelance writers can build a successful career as a writer and earn a consistent income.

Virtual tutoring: You can offer online tutoring services in various subjects and earn money through platforms such as TutorMe or Chegg.

Virtual tutoring is a popular way to earn money online by offering academic assistance to students through video conferencing and other online tools. With the increasing demand for online education, virtual tutoring has become an attractive option for individuals who have expertise in a particular subject and want to share their knowledge with others. Virtual tutoring can be done through various platforms such as TutorMe, Chegg, or even independently through personal connections.

To become a virtual tutor, you need to have expertise in a particular subject or subjects and the ability to effectively communicate and teach others. It's important to identify your target audience and determine the specific subject areas in which you can provide assistance. For example, you might specialize in math, science, English, or test preparation.

Once you have identified your area of expertise, you can create a profile on tutoring platforms such as TutorMe or Chegg. These platforms connect you with students who are seeking academic assistance in your subject area. You can set your own rates and availability and communicate with students through the platform's video conferencing tools.

One of the benefits of virtual tutoring is the flexibility it offers. You can work from anywhere with an internet connection and set your own schedule. This makes it an ideal option for individuals who have other commitments, such as a full-time job or family responsibilities. Additionally, virtual tutoring allows you to work with students from all over the world, expanding your potential client base.

Another benefit of virtual tutoring is the potential to earn a competitive income. Rates vary depending on the subject, experience, and platform used, but virtual tutors can earn anywhere from $20 to $100 per hour.

Additionally, virtual tutors can work with multiple students simultaneously, increasing their earning potential.

However, there are also some challenges to virtual tutoring. One challenge is the need to establish credibility and attract clients. With so many virtual tutors available, it's important to market yourself effectively and provide high-quality services to build a positive reputation. Additionally, virtual tutoring requires a strong internet connection and reliable technology, as technical difficulties can interrupt the tutoring session.

In conclusion, virtual tutoring is a flexible and lucrative way to earn money online by sharing your expertise and knowledge with students who need academic assistance. With the increasing demand for online education, virtual tutoring is becoming an attractive option for individuals who have expertise in a particular subject and want to earn a competitive income. While there are challenges to virtual tutoring, with dedication and effort, virtual tutors can build a successful and fulfilling career as an online tutor.

Online selling: You can start your own online store on platforms like Etsy or eBay and sell handmade or vintage items.

Online selling is a popular way to earn money online by starting your own online store and selling products through platforms such as Etsy or eBay. With the increasing demand for online shopping, online selling has become an attractive option for individuals who have a creative hobby or a collection of vintage items that they want to sell.

To get started with online selling, you need to identify the products that you want to sell and determine your target audience. You can sell handmade products, vintage items, or even digital products such as eBooks or printables. It's important to research the market and identify the trends and demand for your chosen product.

Once you have identified your products, you can create an online store on platforms such as Etsy or eBay. These platforms provide a marketplace where you can list your products, set your own prices, and communicate with customers. It's important to create high-quality product listings with clear descriptions and photographs to attract potential buyers.

One of the benefits of online selling is the potential to reach a global audience. With the internet, you can sell your products to customers from all over the world, expanding your potential customer base. Additionally, online selling allows you to work from anywhere with an internet connection, giving you the flexibility to manage your store around other commitments.

Another benefit of online selling is the potential to earn a competitive income. While earnings vary depending on the type of product and the platform used, online sellers can earn anywhere from a few hundred to several thousand dollars per month. Additionally, online selling allows you to set your own prices and control your profit margins.

However, there are also some challenges to online selling. One challenge is the competition from other online sellers, as the market can be highly saturated with sellers from all over the world. It's important to establish a unique brand and differentiate yourself from competitors to attract customers. Additionally, online selling requires time and effort to manage inventory, shipping, and customer service.

In conclusion, online selling is a flexible and potentially lucrative way to earn money online by selling your products through platforms such as Etsy or eBay. With the increasing demand for online shopping, online selling has become an attractive option for individuals who have a creative hobby or a collection of vintage items that they want to sell. While there are challenges to online selling, with dedication and effort, online sellers can build a successful and fulfilling career as an online entrepreneur.

Online course creation: Create an online course on a topic that you are knowledgeable about and earn money through platforms like Udemy or Skillshare.

Online course creation is a popular way to earn money online by sharing your knowledge and expertise with others. With the increasing demand for online education, online course creation has become an attractive option for individuals who have expertise in a particular subject and want to teach others.

To create an online course, you need to identify the topic that you want to teach and determine your target audience. You can teach anything from programming languages to marketing strategies or even personal development. It's important to research the market and identify the demand for your chosen topic.

Once you have identified your topic, you can create an online course on platforms such as Udemy or Skillshare. These platforms provide a marketplace where you can upload your course, set your own prices, and communicate with students. It's important to create a high-quality course with clear instructions, engaging content, and interactive elements to provide a positive learning experience for students.

One of the benefits of online course creation is the potential to reach a global audience. With the internet, you can teach your course to students from all over the world, expanding your potential customer base. Additionally, online course creation allows you to work from anywhere with an internet connection, giving you the flexibility to manage your course around other commitments.

Another benefit of online course creation is the potential to earn a competitive income. While earnings vary depending on the platform used and the demand for your course, online course creators can earn anywhere from a few hundred to several thousand dollars per month. Additionally, online course creators can earn passive income by selling their course even after it's been created.

However, there are also some challenges to online course creation. One challenge is the need to create high-quality content that provides value to students. With so many online courses available, it's important to differentiate yourself from competitors and create a course that stands out. Additionally, online course creation requires time and effort to create, market, and maintain the course.

In conclusion, online course creation is a flexible and potentially lucrative way to earn money online by sharing your knowledge and expertise with others. With the increasing demand for online education, online course creation has become an attractive option for individuals who have expertise in a particular subject and want to teach others. While there are challenges to online course creation, with dedication and effort, online course creators can build a successful and fulfilling career as an online educator.

Content creation: You can create content for social media platforms or blogs and earn money through ad revenue, sponsorships, or product placements.

Content creation has become an increasingly popular way to earn money in recent years, with the rise of social media platforms and the growth of the blogging industry. There are many ways to create content that can earn you money, whether it's through ad revenue, sponsorships, or product placements. In this article, we'll explore some of the ways you can create content and monetize it.

First and foremost, creating content that people want to engage with is essential to building an audience and earning money. This can include anything from writing blog posts to producing videos or creating social media content. The key is to find your niche and create content that speaks to your audience. Whether it's providing helpful tips and tutorials, sharing your personal experiences, or creating entertaining content that people can relate to, the more engagement your content receives, the more likely you are to attract sponsors and advertisers.

One of the most popular ways to monetize content is through ad revenue. This can be done through platforms such as Google AdSense, which allows you to place ads on your website or blog. When visitors click on these ads, you earn a commission. While this can be a lucrative way to earn money, it can also take time to build up enough traffic to your website or blog to make a significant income.

Sponsorships are another way to monetize your content. This involves working with a company or brand that is relevant to your niche and creating content that promotes their products or services. This can be done through sponsored blog posts, social media posts, or even videos. The key is to ensure that the content feels authentic and fits in with your brand, as this will help to build trust with your audience.

Product placements are another way to monetize your content. This involves working with a brand to feature their products in your content. This can be done through product reviews, unboxing videos, or even including the products in your social media posts. Again, it's important to ensure that the content feels authentic and fits in with your brand.

In addition to these methods, there are many other ways to monetize your content. For example, you can create and sell digital products such as ebooks, courses, or printables. You can also offer coaching or consulting services related to your niche.

Ultimately, the key to monetizing your content is to focus on creating quality content that resonates with your audience. By building a loyal following, you'll be able to attract sponsors, advertisers, and customers who are willing to pay for your products and services. It's important to remember that building a successful content creation business takes time and effort, but with persistence and dedication, you can turn your passion into a profitable venture.

Online consulting: If you have expertise in a specific field, you can offer online consulting services to clients through platforms like Clarity or JustAnswer.

Online consulting has become an increasingly popular way for experts to share their knowledge and earn money from their skills. With the rise of technology and the internet, it's now easier than ever to connect with clients and offer your expertise in a variety of fields. If you have a specific area of expertise, there are several platforms that allow you to offer online consulting services to clients, such as Clarity and JustAnswer.

Clarity is a platform that connects entrepreneurs and small business owners with experts in various fields, including marketing, sales, and finance. As a consultant on Clarity, you set your own rates and clients can book time with you for a phone or video call. Clarity takes a 15% commission on each call, but you keep the rest of the revenue. The platform also offers a feature where clients can leave reviews, which can help you build your reputation and attract new clients.

JustAnswer is another platform that allows experts to offer online consulting services to clients. This platform is more focused on providing answers to specific questions, rather than offering longer consultations. Clients ask a question and you provide a response, either in writing or through a phone call. JustAnswer takes a percentage of the fee, which is set by the platform based on the complexity of the question.

There are several advantages to offering online consulting services. First and foremost, it allows you to share your expertise with a wider audience. You can connect with clients from all over the world and help them solve their problems or achieve their goals. Online consulting also offers flexibility, as you can work from anywhere with an internet connection. This means you can work from home, a coffee shop, or even while traveling.

In addition to these benefits, online consulting can also be a lucrative way to earn money. The fees charged by consultants on these platforms can vary, but many experts charge upwards of $100 per hour for their services. If you have a specific area of expertise that is in high demand, you can potentially earn a significant income from online consulting.

However, it's important to note that online consulting does require some effort and dedication to be successful. You'll need to market your services and build a reputation as an expert in your field. This can be done by creating a professional website, building a social media presence, and engaging with potential clients on the platforms you choose to use. Additionally, you'll need to be responsive and reliable when it comes to scheduling calls and providing advice to clients.

In conclusion, online consulting can be a rewarding and lucrative way for experts to share their knowledge and earn money from their skills. Whether you choose to offer your services on Clarity, JustAnswer, or another platform, it's important to focus on providing high-quality advice and building a positive reputation in your field. With dedication and effort, online consulting can be a successful and fulfilling career path.

Online bookkeeping: You can offer online bookkeeping and accounting services to small businesses and entrepreneurs.

Online bookkeeping and accounting services have become increasingly popular over the years, as more and more small businesses and entrepreneurs seek to outsource their financial tasks to experts. By offering online bookkeeping services, you can help small business owners manage their finances, while also earning money from your skills and expertise.

There are several advantages to offering online bookkeeping services. First and foremost, it allows you to work from anywhere with an internet connection. This means you can work from home, a coffee shop, or even while traveling. You also have the ability to work with clients from all over the world, expanding your potential client base.

To get started with offering online bookkeeping services, you'll need to have some knowledge and experience in the field of bookkeeping and accounting. This may include understanding basic accounting principles, knowledge of accounting software such as QuickBooks, and experience with financial statements and reports.

Once you have the necessary knowledge and experience, you can start to market your services to potential clients. This can be done through creating a website or social media presence, networking with other professionals in your industry, and engaging with potential clients through online forums or groups.

When it comes to pricing your services, you can choose to charge an hourly rate or a fixed fee. The amount you charge will depend on your level of expertise, the amount of work required, and the client's budget. It's important to be transparent about your fees and to provide clients with a clear breakdown of the services you will provide.

To offer online bookkeeping services, you'll need to have access to accounting software such as QuickBooks, which allows you to manage your client's financial records remotely. You can also use cloud-based solutions such as Xero or Wave, which allow you to access your client's financial records from anywhere with an internet connection.

In addition to managing financial records, you'll also need to provide clients with financial statements and reports. These may include profit and loss statements, balance sheets, and cash flow statements. By providing clients with accurate and up-to-date financial reports, you can help them make informed decisions about their business and ensure that they are staying on track financially.

When it comes to working with clients, it's important to be responsive and reliable. This means being available to answer questions and provide advice when needed, as well as providing timely and accurate financial reports. Building a positive reputation with clients can help you attract new business and grow your client base over time.

One of the key benefits of offering online bookkeeping services is that it allows small business owners to focus on other aspects of their business. By outsourcing their financial tasks to experts, they can free up time to focus on sales, marketing, and other important tasks. This can ultimately lead to increased profitability and growth for their business.

In conclusion, online bookkeeping and accounting services can be a lucrative and rewarding career path for those with the necessary knowledge and experience. By offering your services online, you can work from anywhere with an internet connection, while also helping small business owners manage their finances and grow their business. If you have a passion for numbers and a desire to help others, online bookkeeping services may be the perfect career path for you.

Online programming: If you have programming skills, you can offer online programming services to clients through platforms like Upwork or Freelancer.

Online programming services are in high demand as more businesses are moving online and require skilled programmers to develop their websites and applications. If you have programming skills, you can offer your services online and work from anywhere in the world.

To get started with offering online programming services, you'll need to have expertise in a programming language such as Python, Java, JavaScript, or Ruby. You may also need to have knowledge of web development frameworks such as

AngularJS, ReactJS, or VueJS, and database management systems like MySQL, PostgreSQL, or MongoDB.

Once you have the necessary knowledge and expertise, you can start marketing your services to potential clients. You can create a profile on freelancing platforms like Upwork or Freelancer, where businesses post projects and hire freelancers. You can also create a website to showcase your portfolio and services.

When it comes to pricing your services, you can choose to charge an hourly rate or a fixed fee for each project. The amount you charge will depend on your level of expertise, the complexity of the project, and the client's budget. It's important to be transparent about your fees and to provide clients with a clear breakdown of the services you will provide.

One of the advantages of offering online programming services is that you can work with clients from all over the world. This expands your potential client base and allows you to work on a wide range of projects. You also have the flexibility to work from anywhere, as long as you have an internet connection.

To offer online programming services, you'll need to have access to a computer and programming tools like Integrated Development Environments (IDEs) and code editors. You may also need to use version control tools like Git to manage code changes and collaborate with other developers.

When working with clients, it's important to communicate effectively and keep them updated on the progress of their project. This may include providing regular updates, sharing code snippets, and conducting regular meetings to discuss project requirements and progress. It's also important to be responsive to client feedback and make changes as needed to ensure that the project meets their expectations.

One of the key benefits of offering online programming services is that you can specialize in a specific area of programming. For example, you may specialize in web development, mobile app development, or data science. This can help you build a reputation as an expert in your field and attract clients who require your specific expertise.

In conclusion, online programming services can be a lucrative and rewarding career path for those with programming skills and expertise. By offering your services online, you can work from anywhere in the world, expand your potential client base, and specialize in a specific area of programming. If you have a passion for programming and a desire to work independently, online programming services may be the perfect career path for you.

Online graphic design: If you have graphic design skills, you can offer online design services to clients through platforms like 99designs or DesignCrowd.

Online graphic design services are in high demand as businesses are increasingly in need of visual content for their online and offline marketing efforts. If you have graphic design skills, you can offer your services online and work from anywhere in the world.

To get started with offering online graphic design services, you'll need to have expertise in graphic design software such as Adobe Photoshop, Illustrator, or InDesign. You may also need to have knowledge of user experience (UX) design principles and web design best practices.

Once you have the necessary knowledge and expertise, you can start marketing your services to potential clients. You can create a profile on graphic design platforms like 99designs or DesignCrowd, where businesses post design contests and hire designers to create their visual content. You can also create a website to showcase your portfolio and services.

When it comes to pricing your services, you can choose to charge a fixed fee for each project or participate in design contests where the client sets the prize amount. The amount you charge will depend on your level of expertise, the complexity of the project, and the client's budget. It's important to be transparent about your fees and to provide clients with a clear breakdown of the services you will provide.

One of the advantages of offering online graphic design services is that you can work with clients from all over the world. This expands your potential client base and allows you to work on a wide range of projects. You also have the flexibility to work from anywhere, as long as you have an internet connection.

To offer online graphic design services, you'll need to have access to a computer and graphic design software. You may also need to use tools like Dropbox or Google Drive to share files with clients and collaborate with other designers.

When working with clients, it's important to communicate effectively and keep them updated on the progress of their project. This may include providing regular updates, sharing design concepts and drafts, and conducting regular meetings to discuss project requirements and progress. It's also important to be responsive to client feedback and make changes as needed to ensure that the design meets their expectations.

One of the key benefits of offering online graphic design services is that you can specialize in a specific area of design. For example, you may specialize in branding and logo design, web design, or social media graphics. This can help you build a reputation as an expert in your field and attract clients who require your specific expertise.

Another advantage of offering online graphic design services is that you can work on a variety of projects, from small business logos to large-scale marketing campaigns. This allows you to diversify your portfolio and gain experience in a range of design styles and industries.

However, one of the challenges of offering online graphic design services is the competition. With so many designers offering their services online, it can be difficult to stand out from the crowd. To overcome this challenge, it's important to create a strong portfolio that showcases your unique style and expertise. You can also offer personalized services, such as consultations or custom design packages, to differentiate yourself from other designers.

In conclusion, online graphic design services can be a lucrative and rewarding career path for those with graphic design skills and expertise. By offering your services online, you can work from anywhere in the world, expand your potential client base, and specialize in a specific area of design. If you have a passion for graphic design and a desire to work independently, online graphic design services may be the perfect career path for you.

Online language tutoring: You can offer online language tutoring services to people learning a new language through platforms like Italki or Verbling.

Online language tutoring is a popular way to earn money by sharing your language skills with people who are interested in learning a new language. Whether you are fluent in a foreign language or a native speaker, you can use online platforms like Italki or Verbling to offer language tutoring services to people all over the world.

To get started with online language tutoring, you will need to choose a language you are proficient in and create a profile on a tutoring platform. Your profile should include your teaching experience, qualifications, and the hourly rate you charge for your services. You may also need to complete a proficiency test to demonstrate your language skills.

When it comes to pricing your services, you can choose to charge by the hour or offer packages for a set number of lessons. The amount you charge will depend on your level of expertise and the demand for the language you are teaching. It's important to be transparent about your fees and provide clients with a clear breakdown of the services you will provide.

One of the benefits of offering online language tutoring services is that you can work with clients from all over the world. This allows you to reach a wider audience and work with students who are passionate about learning the language you are teaching. You can also work from anywhere in the world, as long as you have an internet connection.

To offer online language tutoring services, you'll need to have access to a computer and a reliable internet connection. You may also need to use tools like Skype or Zoom to communicate with clients and conduct lessons. It's important to have a quiet and distraction-free environment for your lessons to ensure that your students can focus and learn effectively.

When working with clients, it's important to be patient and understanding, especially if they are new to the language. You may need to adapt your teaching style to meet the needs of different students and use a range of teaching methods to keep them engaged and motivated. It's also important to be flexible and accommodate your clients' schedules, as many students may have work or other commitments.

One of the challenges of offering online language tutoring services is the competition. With so many tutors offering their services online, it can be difficult to stand out from the crowd. To overcome this challenge, it's important to create a strong profile that showcases your teaching experience and qualifications. You can also offer personalized services, such as conversation practice or cultural immersion, to differentiate yourself from other tutors.

Another challenge of offering online language tutoring services is building a client base. It may take time to attract clients and build a reputation as a trusted and reliable tutor. However, by providing quality lessons and building a positive relationship with your students, you can attract new clients through word-of-mouth referrals and positive reviews.

In conclusion, online language tutoring is a rewarding and flexible way to earn money by sharing your language skills with others. By offering your services online, you can work with clients from all over the world, work from anywhere, and specialize in a specific language. If you have a passion for teaching and a desire to help others learn a new language, online language tutoring may be the perfect career path for you.

Amazon Affiliate Marketing: Amazon has a massive affiliate program that allows anyone to promote Amazon products and earn a commission on sales. You can sign up for Amazon's affiliate program, and once approved, you can create custom affiliate links for any product on Amazon's website. When someone clicks on your link and makes a purchase, you earn a percentage of the sale.

Sell on Amazon Marketplace: You can sell your own products on Amazon's marketplace. This is a great way to reach a massive audience and leverage Amazon's customer base. You can sell just about anything on Amazon, including physical products, digital products, and services.

Amazon Mechanical Turk: Amazon Mechanical Turk is a marketplace where you can complete small tasks for pay. These tasks can range from data entry to surveys to product categorization. The pay is typically low, but the tasks are usually straightforward and can be completed quickly.

Amazon Kindle Direct Publishing: If you're a writer, you can publish your books on Amazon's Kindle Direct Publishing platform. This platform allows you to sell your books as ebooks on Amazon's website. You can earn up to 70% royalty on your book sales.

Amazon Merch: Amazon Merch is a platform that allows you to design and sell your own t-shirts on Amazon's website. This is a great way to monetize your creativity and earn passive income.

Amazon Handmade: If you're an artist or a crafter, you can sell your handmade products on Amazon Handmade. This is a great way to reach a wider audience and sell your products to people who may not have found them otherwise.

Amazon Flex: Amazon Flex is a program that allows you to deliver packages for Amazon. You can work as much or as little as you want, and you can earn up to $25 per hour.

Amazon Associates Program: Amazon Associates Program is similar to Amazon Affiliate Marketing, but instead of promoting individual products, you promote Amazon Prime memberships. When someone signs up for a Prime membership through your link, you earn a commission.

Amazon FBA: Amazon FBA is a program that allows you to sell your products on Amazon and use Amazon's fulfillment centers to store and ship your products. This program is great for people who want to sell physical products but don't want to deal with the hassle of storing and shipping products themselves.

Amazon Music: Amazon Music is a music streaming service that allows you to upload and sell your music on Amazon's website. This is a great way to reach a wider audience and monetize your music.

Overall, there are many ways to make money with Amazon. Whether you're a writer, an artist, a crafter, or just looking to earn some extra cash, Amazon has something for everyone. Just remember to do your research and choose the program that's right for you.

Writer:

Suleiman Bediev

www.ingramcontent.com/pod-product-compliance
Lightning Source LLC
Chambersburg PA
CBHW041945240526
45473CB00033B/607